D1274575

Quiz # 45654
B. L. 4.7
Pts. 0.5

Great Social Studies Projects™

Pilgrims and Native Americans

Hands-on Projects About Life in Early America

Jennifer Quasha

The Rosen Publishing Group's
PowerKids Press™
New York

Some of the projects in this book were designed for a child to do together with an adult.

For Todd, in memory of the days filled with playing cowgirls and Indians.

Published in 2001 by The Rosen Publishing Group, Inc.
29 East 21st Street, New York, NY 10010

First Edition

Book Design: Felicity Erwin

Layout: Michael de Guzman

Photo Credits: p. 4 © SuperStock; pp. 6 – 21 by Pablo Maldonado.

Quasha, Jennifer.
    Pilgrims and Native Americans : hands-on projects about life in colonial America / Jennifer Quasha.— 1st ed.
      p. cm.— (Great social studies projects)
    Includes index.
    Summary: Projects and activities which highlight the history of the Pilgrims and the Indians in Plymouth Colony.
    ISBN 0-8239-5700-4 (alk. paper)
    1. Pilgrims (New Plymouth Colony)—Study and teaching—Activity programs—Juvenile literature. 2. Massachusetts—History—New Plymouth, 1620–1691—Study and teaching—Activity programs—Juvenile literature. 3. Indians of North America—Massachusetts—History—17th Century—Study and teaching—Activity programs—Juvenile literature. [1. Pilgrims (New Plymouth Colony) 2. Indians of North America—Massachusetts. 3. Massachusetts—History—New Plymouth, 1620–1691. 4. Handicraft.] I. Title.

F68 .Q37 2000
974.4'8202—dc21
                                                                   00-028008

Manufactured in the United States of America

Contents

Pilgrims and Native Americans

The **Pilgrims** were not the first people to make their home in America. When the Pilgrims landed, they found Native Americans already living there. It was not long before the Native Americans made themselves known to the people who had arrived on their land. Though it was not always easy, the Pilgrims and the Native Americans realized that they could learn things from each other, even though they lived very different lives.

One Indian named Squanto was very helpful to the Pilgrims. Squanto taught the Pilgrims how to grow food so they could **survive** in a land that was strange and new to them.

The first Thanksgiving was celebrated by Pilgrims and Native Americans, most likely in 1621.

5

"Stained Glass" Mayflower

On September 6, 1620, a ship called the *Mayflower* left Southampton, England, for America. The ship carried Pilgrims who wanted **religious** freedom. The ship had three **masts** and was 106 feet (32.3 m) long. It traveled at about two miles (3.2 km) per hour and only covered around 53 miles (85.3 km) a day. The *Mayflower* spent 66 days at sea. Here's how to make your own *Mayflower*:

tools and materials

- two pieces of black construction paper
- thick pile of newspapers
- gold crayon
- X-Acto knife or scissors
- clear tape
- one piece each of blue, red, white, and brown tissue paper

Stack two pieces of black construction paper on top of the newspapers. With gold crayon draw the shapes (see picture) that make up the ship.

 Carefully, with the X-Acto knife or scissors, cut out the shapes from the black paper. Keep the pieces of black paper stacked.

 Set aside the bottom piece of black paper (the one without crayon marks). Tape colored tissue paper onto the top sheet as shown.

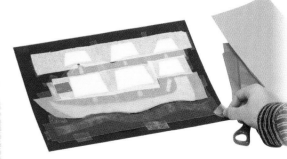

 Take the second piece of black paper and place it on top, so the two pieces line up. Tape the two pieces together.

Try On a Pilgrim Hat

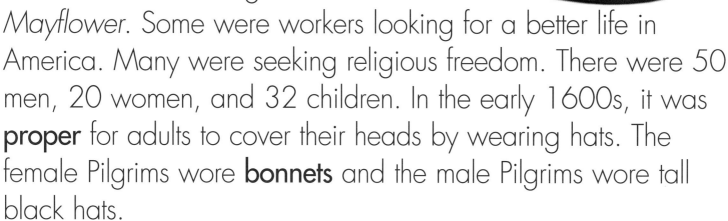

There were 102 Pilgrims aboard the *Mayflower*. Some were workers looking for a better life in America. Many were seeking religious freedom. There were 50 men, 20 women, and 32 children. In the early 1600s, it was **proper** for adults to cover their heads by wearing hats. The female Pilgrims wore **bonnets** and the male Pilgrims wore tall black hats.

Here's how to make your own Pilgrim hat:

<table>
<tr><td>tools and materials</td><td>
<ul>
<li>one 22" x 28" (57 x 71cm) sheet of black poster board</li>
<li>scissors</li>
<li>stapler</li>
<li>one sheet of brown construction paper</li>
<li>gold crayon</li>
<li>masking tape</li>
<li>one piece of yellow felt</li>
</ul>
</td></tr>
</table>

1 Cut a piece of black poster board that measures 12 inches (30.5 cm) wide. Roll up until it is correct size to fit around your head. Make top hole smaller than opening that fits around head. Staple together. Trim top and bottom openings to make them level.

2 On the other piece of poster board, with a gold crayon, trace two circles the size of the top and bottom openings. Draw a circle two inches (5 cm) wide around the large circle for a brim.

3 Cut around the inner and outer circles of the larger circle. This will become the hat brim. Then cut out smaller circle (for hat top).

4 Tape small circle to the top of the hat. Put tape on inside of hat. Tape brim in place. Cut brown band from paper and yellow buckle from felt. Tape them on.

Native American Headdress

The way the Native Americans lived and dressed was new to the Pilgrims. For example, Native Americans used many different types of **headdresses**. The headdresses were used for **decoration** and in religious **ceremonies** and dances. The Native Americans used feathers, bones, shells, and animal skins to decorate the headdresses. Here's how to make your own Native American headdress:

tools and materials

- one piece each of red, yellow, green, and blue construction paper
- scissors
- stapler
- feathers
- glue
- sequins

1 Cut a two-inch (5-cm) long strip of red construction paper that will fit around your head. This will be a headband. If necessary, staple two strips of paper together to make it long enough. Cut out construction paper feathers.

2 Staple construction paper feathers to the headband. Then staple real feathers to the headband.

3 Glue sequins to the bottom of headpiece.

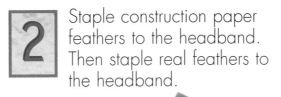

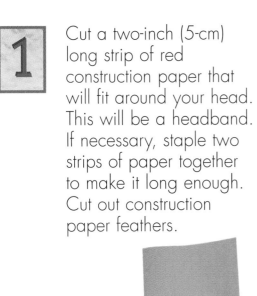

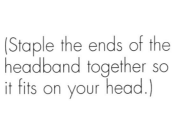

(Staple the ends of the headband together so it fits on your head.)

Make a Pilgrim Ornament

The Pilgrims were sometimes called Separatists. The Pilgrims came from England. In England, anyone who did not follow the beliefs of the Church of England was considered "separate." The Pilgrims were considered separate because they did not hold the same beliefs as most English people did. The Pilgrims wore plain, simple clothes unlike many English people. Here's how to make your own Pilgrim ornament:

tools and materials

- one sheet of black poster board
- scissors
- one piece of white construction paper
- one piece of yellow construction paper
- clear tape
- wallet-sized photo of yourself— cut out your head only
- single-hole puncher
- eight-inch (20.3-cm) piece of yarn

Cut out a seven-inch (17.8-cm) tall male or female figure from the black poster board.

Cut pieces needed for your Pilgrim clothes. Cut out the apron, bonnet, cuffs, and collars from the white paper, and a belt buckle from the yellow paper.

Tape your cut-out photo to the body of the Pilgrim. Then add either the hat or the bonnet.

Punch a single hole into the hat or bonnet and tie an eight-inch (20.3-cm) piece of yarn to hang the Pilgrim ornament.

Shake a Native American Rattle

Rattles were very important to Native Americans. They used them during their religious ceremonies and dances. Native Americans also had doctors called "medicine men." Often these medicine men would use the rattles during **healing rituals** when someone was sick. The rattles were usually made from buffalo horns, turtle shells, animal skins, and wood. Here's how to make your own Native American rattle:

tools and materials	
• a clean, empty tin can	• scissors
• masking tape	• four pennies
• white glue	• four pebbles
• dowel	• duct tape
• pencil	• feathers
• one piece each of red and green construction paper	

Place four strips of masking tape over the opening of the tin can. Leave a hole in the center of the can. Place a dab of glue on the end of the dowel. Place the dowel through center hole. Let dry overnight.

 With the pencil, trace the bottom of the can on a piece of construction paper and cut out the circle. Fold circle in half and cut a small opening in the center that will fit around dowel. Cut out construction paper decorations.

 Place pennies and pebbles in can. Then, with duct tape, tape construction paper circle on the top of the can and around the dowel.

 Decorate the rattle any way you like by using feathers and construction paper.

Pilgrim Family Finger-Puppets

Life was hard for the Pilgrims. On December 25, 1620, nine days after the *Mayflower* arrived in Plymouth Harbor, the Pilgrims began building their first house. Until their houses were ready, the Pilgrim families lived on the *Mayflower*. Their first winter in America was long, cold, and very hard. Here's how to make your own finger-puppet Pilgrim family:

tools and materials

- one kitchen glove (from a pair) (black kitchen gloves work best)
- scissors
- one piece each of white and yellow felt
- yellow and brown yarn
- white glue
- googly eyes
- one sheet of black construction paper

Take a kitchen glove and cut four fingers off of it. Cut two small aprons, two bonnets, and four white collars from white felt. These should be sized to fit the glove fingers. Cut two buckles from the yellow felt. Cut yarn to make hair.

From black construction paper, cut two, one-inch (2.5-cm) long strips and roll each tightly to make hats for the male Pilgrims. Glue each roll together. When dry, make three small cuts around the bottoms of each roll and fold paper out to make the brims of the hats. Glue hats onto top of male puppets.

Glue all of the above to the cut-off glove fingers. When dry, add eyes.

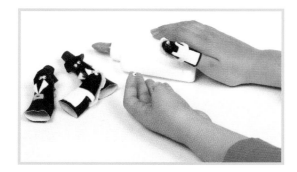

Indian Ring Game

The Native Americans worked very hard to survive and keep their communities strong. The grown-ups had to provide food and homes for themselves and their children. When they had free time, they enjoyed playing games. The children especially liked to play games that tested their **hand-eye coordination**, like ring games. Here's how to make your own Indian ring game:

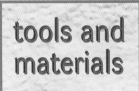

tools and materials

- cardboard
- scissors
- X-Acto knife
- one piece of balsa wood that is: 8″ x 4″x 1/8″ (20.3 x 10.2 x 0.3 cm)
- two-foot (61-cm) piece of black yarn
- white glue
- one piece of balsa wood that is: 8″x3/4″x1/4″ (20.3 x 1.9 x 0.6 cm)

- red, white & black construction paper
- black marker
- two empty key rings

1 Cut two four-inch (10-cm) circles from cardboard. Use an X-Acto knife to cut "horns" from the wider piece of wood.

2 Wrap yarn four times around center of horns. Glue yarn to horn, then glue horn to one cardboard circle. Leave most of the yarn hanging down. Glue on the long, thin piece of wood for the handle.

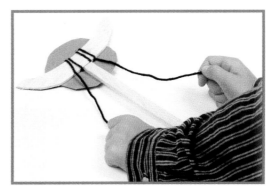

3 Glue on other cardboard circle to the other side. Cut out a paper circle the same size as cardboard one. Decorate the paper circle.

4 Glue "face" to cardbord. Tie one key ring to each piece of yarn about 10 inches (25.4 cm) from horn. Now try to flip the rings so they hook on horns.

Thanksgiving Mobile

We celebrate Thanksgiving to remember a three-day **harvest** festival that historians think took place in the fall of 1621. The feast was shared by both Pilgrims and Native Americans. Many of the foods we eat on Thanksgiving, like turkey, squash, and corn, are foods that the Pilgrims and Native Americans ate at their feast. Here's how to make a Thanksgiving mobile that includes images from the feast:

tools and materials

- blue, yellow, green, and red construction paper
- one hanger
- scissors
- clear tape
- pencil
- single-hole puncher
- black yarn

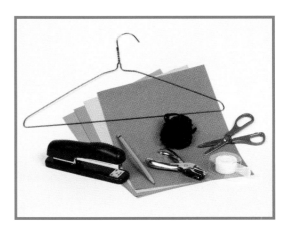

Stack pieces of green, red, yellow, and blue construction paper on top of each other. Trace half of the hanger and cut shape out.

 Tape two of the shapes together then repeat with the other colors. This will be the hanger cover at the end.

 Using the rest of the construction paper, draw and cut out images like a turkey, corn, apples, Pilgrims, and pumpkins. Tape each of these images onto square pieces of construction paper that you have cut out.

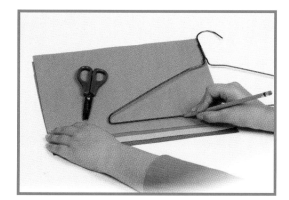

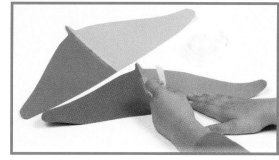

 Punch a hole at the top of each square piece of paper and tie to the hanger with yarn. Place hanger cover over hanger.

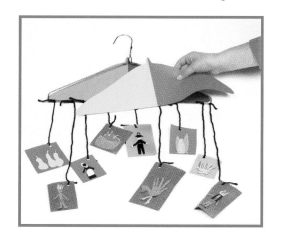

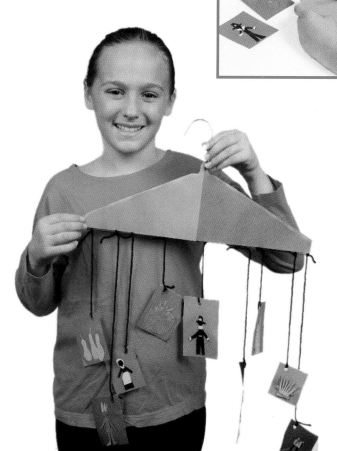

Using Your Projects

Now you've learned some interesting facts about the Pilgrims and Native Americans who lived in the early days of America. You've made some terrific projects, too. There are lots of things you can do with them. You can give them away as presents. The Thanksgiving mobile would be a nice way to thank your parents for preparing a tasty Thanksgiving meal. Maybe you can show your little sister or brother how to use the Indian ring game. The Pilgrim finger-puppet family might come in handy for a school project.

The things you have made can also make nice decorations for your kitchen refrigerator! Frame, hang, or display them any way you like, but make sure you share your great social studies projects, and the knowledge you've learned, with your family and friends.

Glossary

bonnets (BAH-nits) Cloth or straw hats, worn by women and children, that tie under the chin with a ribbon.

ceremonies (SEHR-ih-moh-neez) Special series of acts that are done on certain occasions.

decoration (deh-kuh-RAY-shun) An object or design that makes something prettier.

hand-eye coordination (HAND-IY kew-or-dih-NAY-shun) Being able to move your hand quickly and easily exactly the way you want to move it.

harvest (HAR-vist) A season's gathered crop.

headdresses (HED-dres-iz) Cloths or decorations worn on the head.

healing rituals (HEEL-ing RIH-chu-wulz) Ceremonies done to make sick people better.

masts (MASTS) Tall poles that hold up the sails of a ship.

Pilgrims (PIL-grimz) People who came to America from England in 1620 on the *Mayflower*.

proper (PRAH-pur) Right or correct.

religious (ree-LIH-jus) Having to do with a religion, or a system of spiritual beliefs.

survive (sur-VYV) To stay alive.

23

Index

Web Sites

To learn more about Pilgrims and Native Americans in early America, check out this Web site:

http://www.thewaters.org/columns/thanksgiving.html